TOWARDS A BLISS

NONE

SONAM TOPWAL

Made with ♥ on the Notion Press Platform
www.notionpress.com

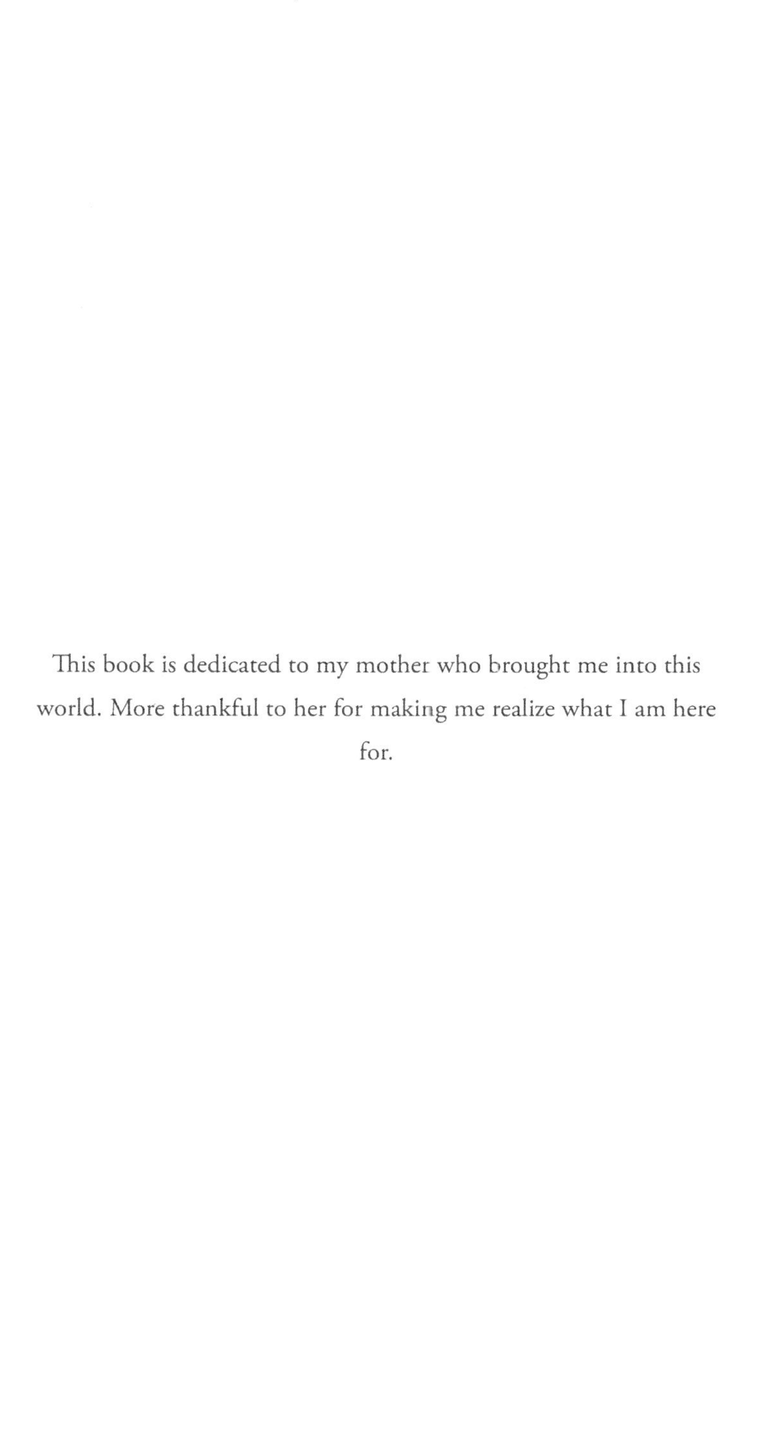

This book is dedicated to my mother who brought me into this world. More thankful to her for making me realize what I am here for.

Contents

Foreword

I taught her to be independent and always left her free to share her thoughts. She was always active in all that was happening around her and actively presented her thoughts on various concerns across different platforms. I feel very happy that she is here for a positive change through her words while teaching and writing.

-Vinita Topwal

Preface

The reason for writing this collection of poems lies in bringing a positive change in society. We as humans discriminate on various parameters like gender, caste, religion etc. Also, the majority of people are not putting efforts in the right direction to achieve success. This book through its poems attempts to show the real path of happiness and thatswhy titled, "Towards a Bliss" Enjoy turning the pages of the bliss.

Acknowledgements

I would like to thank all those who motivated me to do something for the betterment of the entire human race. In this journey of life, till now have faced many who tried to put an end to my happy journey, but all those who were there are still there and will be there forever. For, they put humanity first.

Chapter1

Revered Cities

The snow has enveloped the buzzing hymns.
With the gelid ice flakes averting the wise move.
Reminiscent of the gloomy grey sky narrating a tale of the lost cries.
Those pale countenances engulfing my heart and soul, as
I try to pour a bundle of joy on those sours.
The cities are decorated with baits trapping them in a vicious circle of unending ardour,
they cannot even apologize.
Oh! My mother! why the affluent with power have lost their sight.
Has the value education propagated during ancient times not been revived?
Well!! The indigence of my motherland has ceaselessly agonized my mind.
I beseech the immortal to illuminate the egomaniacal towards solace for the benefit of the entire human race.

Chapter2

An Abandoned Soul

The dawn has arrived with the calm breeze, blowing and making a swift noise, I still look for the light.

Forlorn has grasped my conscience and I feel pitied by the shimmering daylight.

For the day seems like ages, with each moment chiding me for my misery.

I am still a bairn, not knowing the solutions to this torturous plight.

Why am I treated harshly, always berated and admonished for others' plight?

As I walk along the ceaseless journey, my feets get numb, and my heart throbs with enduring pain,

Always asking for an answer for this agony to the supreme light.

Contemplating, I finally get a solution for all the storms, surpassing my all other flights.

I choose to read, I choose to write, I choose to ignite the ripped hopeless souls.

Chapter3

A Delight in the Dazzling Eyes

Those youthful faces narrate an ordeal of unfulfilled wishes weaving a story of destitute.

Who is to be denounced for the hardships and miseries they face?

Menace is decided by the supreme power and who we are to abhor the atrocities they face.

As the chilled wind blows below the iron-grey sky, the hall starts to freeze, but undeterred they remain.

Well! All I see is an unending dream in their dazzling eyes.

Has the miseries ever been able to affect those who know nothing,

more than the real meaning of how dawn and dusk are not alike?

Courage and strength for those tiny souls is all I ask. The heaven may seem far, but life after the toil

will be a blissful delight.

Chapter4

Unending Ardour

Numerous unending sentences they utter,
different plots they weave to derail you from your path of happiness.
Heed no attention to those immature unaware souls, for they do not know what they are here for.
Forgive them for all they do. Remember the supreme is discerning their ill-thoughts.
Why? Oh lord! When they know that others are somewhat better, they degrade you at your back.
Why has the world become so egotistical? Why have the thoughts become so contaminated?
For, I believe we have forgotten the values that ancient wise sages taught us.

Chapter5

Neck of the Woods

How alluring do those walls look, festooned not with the embellished posters of the exemplar,

but with the magical words that engross all the attention.

Welcome to the neck of the woods where words and locutions are coloured with all the shades,

showing an embarking on a ceaseless journey.

Sentiments and experiences harbinger dazzling thoughts which when expelled out of the soul,

create magic called euphoria.

A line read, "I will make you the most resplendent woman in today's fiesta" and the woman replies,

"This will make me feel on top of the world."

The conundrum is a preponderance of women's mentality. Why do a women needs to look great to be accepted?

Knowledge is what every woman needs so that amidst the impermanency of youth, permanent wisdom comes to her rescue.

Chapter6

Glory of Heaven

The gloomy shadows of the two-faced haunted her soul for a long,

but eventually, she came out of it strong.

How long can one agonize? Rip the soul into parts?

Only till one has the power to control your thoughts.

When she feels desolated in this masked world, the supreme almighty makes a rush.

Kind and innocent souls can't be left, the only way to attain heaven is to trust who matters.

"Their deeds, I preserve in an immense canvas and one day do make them realize their deeds by making them helpless.

Eventually, they do realize that God's abode is only the true happiness.

Chapter7

Unending Saudade

How can I not cherish those charming words flowing like a liberated flock of words?

Entering a zone where there are no barriers.

How connected do I feel those heartbeats? which discerns all that I fail to suggest.

Never has anyone been able to understand what I relish, what agonizes my conscience,

Other than my dazzling soul.

I tingle with excitement when those eyes sparkle in my dreams and paint a rainbow of happiness.

For infinity, I can wait to hold those hands that hold me even when I am alone.

I beseech the supreme to give me the firmness to live my old age alone.

Putting all that I always revered in this beautiful world's home.

Chapter8

Echelons of Humans

With folded hands and a throbbing heart, they arrive. asking forbearance.

I scan their minds and an eerie sketch gets revealed, narrating a story of an egomaniacal race.

My feet are decorated with flowers and an array of offerings pour, flooding me with all unending sours.

I feel being bribed but remain a statue discerning a real devotee.

On returning to their abode, a different story is weaved.

They get involved in everything other than what I preach.

Unapologetically, they harm others for their own cause, eat non-veg and

recite O my lord!

Not realizing this will only lead to their distraught, tying them infinitely to this abode.

Chapter9

Earthisism

The wings of my soul unfasten when I breathe.

How can I expound the euphoria of living in this exquisite world?

Blooming fields and dazzling sunlight weave a story, a narrative of

the unending fondness of the great mother safeguarding her child's nourishment.

My eyes lighten up when I discern the verdant valleys with blooming flowers,

alongside the perennial river and alluring waterfalls.

Abrupting, I notice they all being in tears and gently ask why is all and sundry shedding tears.

They retort why our charm and love are being rewarded by making us vulnerable.

Soon our existence will be in trouble and Mother Earth will struggle to endeavour.

Chapter10

Detracted Head

In a sedentary, I observe eternity.

How can the masses be so engrossed?

I ask, but I don't get an answer.

"About a week, you have an exam". An exam of your destiny.

One of the perturbed voices speaks and here you have an answer,

"Its ample time, I would easily prepare"

The jittery voice showing concern, signals, "It's the question of your future"

The other retorts, "My future, not yours"

Where are the masses hooked up? What are they busy searching for?

How intensely I want them to hear the echo of my aching voice.

Posting and chatting to seek attention is not what we are here for.

Our aim in this life should be much higher.

Remember in a distracted head, knowledge cannot gather.

Chapter11

Recital of a Shattered Woman

Lying on a Chesterfield, she recollects her gone past.
How eternity was absorbed in reading and putting life in the worlds
through magical thoughts.
How everything observed her fondly and in return,
how it was decorated on the piece of paper.
Warned, she immediately stands and moves hearing the whining of the baby.
One more voice abrupts, denouncing the food for taste.
How can the world be so callous? She asks the lord.
Support with dignity is all she prays for. Even if help is offered, gibes
and derision are always what she hears deepening her sours.
When she questions, cruel calls, either manage the home or go back to your abode.

Chapter12

Supremacy of Humanity

Merry children along with a whole bunch of friends,
hanging and playing jovially around the school's fence,
with so much happiness and contentment.
Teacher preaching the path of peace and humanity.
I proudly say, my country is so great!!
Homecoming and wandering with mischievous friends,
playing all sorts of wonderful games,
Mom and Dad at home narrating inspirational stories to be read.
Today, I try to find out my friends, my mom and dad, but under the debris,
I find the holy books, making no sense.
I long for the ambrocious delicacies they served with love on the plate in my hands
I beg my dear lord, to give those beautiful moments back.
My dream of becoming a peacekeeper, please don't forget.
Although I am dead.

Chapter13

Boundless Thoughts

With the oaks and the deodars dancing along the high and cool path,
I imagine a place called heaven on earth.
Suddenly, my mind revolves around my research.
Another thought engulfs, were the ghosts and spirits mentioned
in the recently finished novel real.
All of a sudden, I rush to the nearby table, take out one of the novels,
and read one of the character's struggling years.
Amidst all this, I start reading a chapter that has to be taught in tomorrow's lecture.
During this process, several other thoughts trigger.
I Stop and ask, what's the matter?
After a lot of contemplation, I finally get an answer.
Focus on one task at a time forever and nothing will stop you from further.

Chapter14

The Chosen Direction

Flaks, abominations and chides. All this and whatnot I hear.

But still, I remain undeterred.

"Who will take your care when we are nowhere?", my parents murmur.

"The world is full of awful criminals. "How will you sail smooth in this obnoxious air"?

I fail to justify why I am here.

I imagine the masses living in extreme trouble despite being a hard worker,

and a few enjoying life without any trouble.

I ask why so much struggle in a country full of intellectuals.

I always fail to get a true answer.

The workforce remains under extreme pressure, fearing they might lose the job offered.

Despite being 100 others around the corner.

I hope, one day I will get an answer for all the struggles that people of my country suffer.

www.ingramcontent.com/pod-product-compliance
Lightning Source LLC
LaVergne TN
LVHW040939150826
845672LV00008B/2447

* 9 7 9 8 8 9 2 7 7 2 0 0 6 *